MORNING FACE

The schoolboy with his satchel
And shining morning face.

Shakespeare

" If I have moved among my race,
And shown no glorious morning face—"

" Call us up with morning faces."

Stevenson

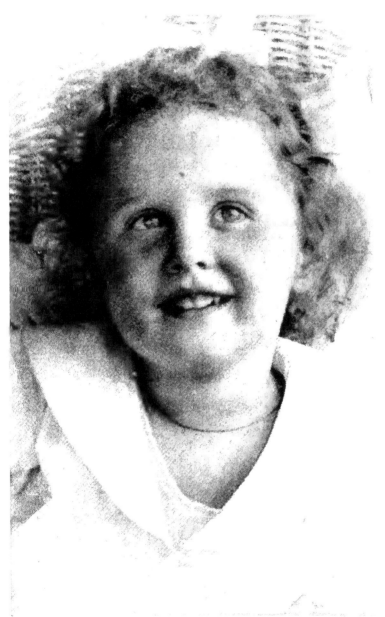

"Call us up with morning faces" —*R. L. S.*

MORNING FACE

WHEN the sun scatters the shadows of night,
Until Kestler's tamaracks turn gold in its light,
When the sky is blue, and the clouds rose-pink,
When the redbird wakens the sleeping chewink,
When dew bejewels the pond lily's face,
While red waves shimmer 'neath silver foam lace,
When rainbows of light are gaily unfurled,
Then, morning has come to the rest of the world.

When its light reaches your little white bed,
Brightening sun-rav'lings that halo your head,
Touching cheeks of wild rose, eyes of sky blue,
The wondering smile that wakens with you,
Your lips line of red, the pearl of your teeth,
The pulsing white throat, the warm body beneath,
Of pain or of trouble, no faintest trace,
There, morning for me, dear, dawns on your face.

Swinging on a grapevine swing,
Hear old Redbird's whistle ring!

MORNING FACE

With Illustrations

BY

GENE STRATTON-PORTER

AUTHOR OF
"THE SONG OF THE CARDINAL," "MOTHS
OF THE LIMBERLOST," "MUSIC OF
THE WILD," "FRECKLES," "THE
HARVESTER," "LADDIE"

GARDEN CITY   NEW YORK
DOUBLEDAY, PAGE & COMPANY
1916

Baby Oriole

Morning Face: "Now Bob, *that* is a serious plant."
  Bob Black: "But what is a 'serious plant,' dear?"
Morning Face: "The kind where Gene looks serious if
  you touch it."

8

DEDICATION

ONE LITTLE GIRL WITH A FACE OF MORNING,
A WONDERING SMILE HER LIPS ADORNING,
WISHES HER PICTURES AND STORIES TO SHARE,
SO SHE SENDS THEM TO CHILDREN, EVERYWHERE

LIST OF BOOKS

CONTENTS

CONTENTS

ILLUSTRATIONS

By Author unless Otherwise
Indicated

ILLUSTRATIONS

14

ILLUSTRATIONS

Joy sailed over the morning's crest,
   Freighting a Mourning Cloak's painted wing,
Straight to its homing place in my breast,
   So my enraptured heart began to sing.

PUBLISHER'S NOTE

A few years ago providence sent for a time, a tiny girl-child into the home of Gene Stratton-Porter, a sunshiny little girl having eyes wide with the marvel and beauty of the world around her, and a heart naturally so full of joy that she invariably awakened from sleep with a wondering smile on her lips, even when so small that it was difficult to differentiate a smile from a muscular cramp. Always, especially tender and brilliant was the morning awakening. Studying the baby with the eyes of love, Mrs. Porter soon noticed this, so the little visitor had been only a few days at the Cabin in Wildflower Woods, when she named her "Morning Face," because the child constantly brought to her mind Stevenson's lines in "The Prayer," "Call us up with morning faces," and from "The Celestial Surgeon":

"If I have moved among my race,
And shown no glorious morning face——"

From the hour of this little girl's birth, Mrs Porter improvised and recited for her amusement endless sing-song chants, rhymes, jingles, or told stories about the flowers, birds, and animals surrounding the Cabin, making amusing pictures to illustrate them When Morning Face was taken East by her parents, she missed

17

her play-fellow and her entertainment, so once a week Mrs. Porter wrote a new story or chant for her, sending it in a letter with the illustration pasted on the back. The day came inevitably when Morning Face demanded that her stories and pictures be made into a book, then later the further request that her book be "made like the other books," so that she could give copies of it to her little relatives and playmates. So the book has been reproduced for all children, exactly as Mrs. Porter designed it for this one child of her heart.

THE BOOK

Mrs. Porter makes no slightest claim to being a poet, or that many of the subjects of this book are poetical. It merely represents her methods of entertaining and teaching natural history to the babies of her own family. Most of the contents were improvised and recited for years before being recorded. When the fact was pointed out to Mrs Porter that some of the chants were irregular in rhythm, she retorted that others were perfect, which proved that she could have made all of them so, had she chosen, but in the constant use of the names of insects, birds, animals, flowers, she would be exact, using only familiar speech, so instead of conforming the words to the metre, in the proper reading of the book, there are places where it becomes necessary to conform the metre to the words. This is the key-note of the book: *it is for the ear; to be read aloud; in many of the rhymed lines the intended and proper effect can be obtained only by chanting*

18

PUBLISHER'S NOTE

*the lines and lengthening or shortening the syllables to fit
the metre, like a rune or incantation.* The book is about
living things, for the most part baby creatures, for which
all children have natural affection. The irregularity of
rhythm, which was designed to make the lines native to
children, was intentional and used for that purpose It
will require only a little practice to enable those reading
to catch the rhythm, so that they will instinctively shorten
or lengthen syllables to fit the metre. So chanted the
book will give to all children the peculiar delight the
little people of Limberlost Cabin find in it

THE ILLUSTRATIONS

In a lifetime of field work in natural history illustration
with half a dozen cameras, operating in different ways;
through making friends with the birds and animals by days
of slow approach and painstaking work, in order to secure
the most characteristic studies possible with which to
illustrate her books on natural history, Mrs. Porter
frequently secured intensely characteristic pictures, cunning pictures, truly speaking likenesses of her wild subjects Whenever such a picture was produced, one that
she regarded as a real triumph, one which sometimes
meant days or weeks of patient approach, again the flash
of the thousandth part of a second, Mrs. Porter laid it
away "to save for something good enough." All of these
pictures go into "Morning Face." It represents the
cream and culmination of a lifetime of field work, which
she hopes will give to all children the joy it has brought to
one little girl she so loves.

Mr. Musk Rat left his 'dobe house,

Screech Owl.

" *Gene, do*
Sing-Song 'Bout

WILDFLOWER WOODS"

LISTEN to old Screech Owl screech,
Down in his house in the big gray beech.
Mister Coon went there to dine,
And stuck his mouth with porcupine.

Swinging on a grapevine swing,
Hear old Redbird's whistle ring!
Hear him cry: "Good cheer, Good cheer!
I live in Gene's woods all the year."

Mister Rattlesnake, down in the grass,
Wouldn't let Mud Turtle pass.
Turtle bit a diamond off his back,
Guinea on the fence cried: "Rack! Pot rack!"

ld Miss Swallow wanted a drink,
lack Bass gobbled her, quick as wink.
.ingfisher watching from a dead tree,
.aughed: "Ha, ha! You can beat me!"

Iissus Field Mouse found a great big
    hole
)ug in her house by Miss Ground Mole.
Look what you've done!" she cried
    in surprise.
'*Look!*'" said Miss Mole. "Without
    any eyes?"

21

Mister Coon

MORNING FACE

Ground Puppy had a crick in his back,
He went to Dr. Duck, a dreadful quack.
Duck cured the pain, but Puppy didn't thrive,
'Cause his doctor ate him alive.

Missus Pewee built her nest 'bove the door,
Red Squirrel threw her eggs on the floor.
When he ran to the closest tree,
Yellow Hammer hammered him com-plete-ly.

"Missus Pewee built her nest 'bove the door."

WILDFLOWER WOODS

Mother Ground Hog stold a cabbage head,
The Paris-green made her sick in bed.
Mr. Ground Hog gave her "pod-o-phyl-lene,"
To counteract the dose of Paris-green.

Old Mr. Musk Rat left his 'dobe house,
On Gene's rarest orchid bed to browse,
Blue Jay cried: "I'm going straight to tell!"
So he rang the big dinner bell.

Gene came flying with the kitchen broom,
Musk Rat hiked back to his closest room.
If I could do just what I really wish,
I'd live there so I could help Grandad fish.

"I'd live there so I could help

"Old Robin brought a slick fishworm,

BREAD AND MILK

EVERY morning before we eat,
My mother prays a prayer sweet.
  With folded hands and low-bowed head.
  "Give us this day our daily bread "
But I'd like tarts and ginger cakes,
Puffs and pie like grandmother makes.
  So 'smorning I said my appetite
  Must have cake, or 'twouldn't eat a bite
Then mother said: "'Fore you get through,
You'll find just bread and milk will do."

She always lets me think things out,
But I went to the yard to pout,
  What I saw there—Upon my word!
  I'm glad I'm a girl,—not a bird
Redbreast pulled up a slick fishworm,
To feed her child: *it ate the squirm*
  Bee-bird came flying close to me,
  And caught a stinging honey bee.
She pushed it down her young, alive
She must have thought him a beehive.

"Bluebirds had worms, where I could see,
For breakfast, in their hollow tree."

"Missus Wren snapped up a spider."

BREAD AND MILK

Old Warbler searched the twigs for slugs,
Rose Grosbeak took potato bugs.
  Missus Wren snapped up a spider,
  To feed her baby, close beside her.
Little Kingbirds began to squall,
Their mother hurried at their call.
  She choked them with dusty millers.
  Cuckoos ate hairy caterpillars.
Blue birds had worms, where I could see,
For breakfast, in their hollow tree.
Then little Heron made me squeal,
  Beside our lake he ate an eel.
When young Screech Owl gulped a whole mouse,
I started fast for our nice house.

Right over me—for pit-tee sake,
Home flew a hawk, with a big snake!
  So 'fore my tummy got awful sick,
  I ran and kissed my mother quick.
I acted just as fine as silk
And asked polite for bread and milk.

27

"Gene, tell 'bout the Indigo Blue Bird."

THE INDIGO BLUE BIRD

'CAUSE we are Indigo Babies you'd think we are blue,
　But we're gray and brown with small touches of white.
　You can see that our tummies are stuffed bursting tight,
　We flew 'way up here from our cradle all right,
And we are going to act big and sleep up here, too!

I am always a good bird and behave most polite,
　But my little Brother is one of the very worst,
　He stretches the tallest and grabs the biggest bug first,
　If he'd swallowed one more worm to-day, he'd have
　　burst,
Mummy says he can be trusted to act a perfect fright.

I couldn't be blamed much, if I'd start family fights,
　Brother is going to be blue, but I got to stay brown.
　He always swallows the biggest, juiciest bites down,
　I think I am the one to squall, scold and frown,
I believe I'll be progressive and vote for women's rights!

28

THE SPIDER'S TRAP

A BIG black spider, homed in my tulip bed,
So that her children might be comfortably fed.
She wove her dainty web, with such cunning art,
Around every stamen in the tulips' heart,
That never a bee, called by the colours gay,
Lived to hunt honey on another fair day.

29

"Gene, tell me 'bout how the flowers were made."

HOW THE FLOWERS WERE MADE

You know, Morning Face, that old Mother Nature made all the pretty things in the world, so of course she made the flowers. You know, too, that the earth is her house, so like every woman, she wanted it to be beautiful. In the beginning of the world she had plain moss green carpet for her floor, green vines, bushes and trees for her walls, with blue, cloud-covered sky for her roof. She had the sun for light by day, the moon was her big lamp at night and each little twinkly star was her candle. The winds were her fan. She had gay colour forever shining on the faces of the seas and lakes, reflected by the sky, the sun, moon, stars, and clouds. Sometimes she had a wonderful rainbow of light all stripes of violet, blue, yellow, and red; but the forests, the fields, and mountains were all some shade of green, while the deserts were gray and sand colour

Now Mother Nature is perfectly beautiful herself. Her hair is yellow as sunshine, her eyes are sky blue, her cheeks cloud pink, while she wears a green silky dress all embroidered in leaves and vines. She knows she is beautiful,

31

so she wants her house beautiful also. She likes the sky and the water best, because of their colour, but she could not live there all the time, for each day her work was filling the earth with butterflies, birds, and animals, so of course, she knew that before very long the little children would be coming.

So one day she sat looking at her green house with its floor and walls all of one colour until she cried: "Mercy me, such a sameness! I wish I could brighten my house up a little before my children come." She looked at the sky and the water a long time, then at the earth; at last, right out loud she said it: "I really believe I shall try." Now when Mother Nature tries to do anything, she usually does such perfectly wonderful things that it takes us years and years to learn how and why she did them

She started slowly flying around the world, gathering all the exquisite colour she could find; big sheets of moonlight, starshine, and heaps of sea foam She took sunshine where it fell from deepest gold to palest yellow, every blue of the sky, armloads of pink and purple clouds with every single rainbow she could find Then she carried them to earth, sat down in the midst of the heap, took out her scissors and began cutting flower faces from them.

32

"She cut tiny ones of misty sea foam for many "

HOW THE FLOWERS WERE MADE

First she tried moonlight and starshine, because she had so much of that. She began on simple, easy ones, cutting little rounded petals that she set in a circle, touching it with her lips in the centre to put in life and add sweetening. Like this! See? When she stuck a few on a little plant at her feet, her lips began to quiver, her eyes to shine, while her shears flashed in

"She made bowls of cupped petals to float on the still waters."

the light, and her fingers flew so fast you could not watch them; because at once she saw what would happen when she had her whole earth-house brightened with different colours and shapes of flowers.

She began with the walls, putting tiny ones of misty sea foam on the cornel and many others, larger ones, on the hawthorne, and big creamy ones on the magnolias. She cut long slender petals for the daisies; stars with snipped edges for the campion. Every one she finished she grew wilder with joy. From pale moonlight she fashioned big snow-white lily trumpets for the fields, while from creamy starshine she made bowls of narrow-cupped petals to float on the still waters. To use up the scraps she made white violets and from the teeniest of all chickweed and dodder bloom.

33

MORNING FACE

Then she began on blue. She had heaps of that because she could take big pieces from the sky and then patch the place with pink clouds, so it really looked better than before   First she cut a few plain, easy petals for hepatica; then she made violets of every shape. The more she made, the more skillful she grew, the lovelier things she could think of to try next, while always her hands flew faster. She thought the blue of the sky the perfect colour, so her heart throbbed, her lips quivered with delight, and her eyes were brighter than the sky, as she began cutting out tiny little tinkly hairbells, and blue bells, bell flowers, and blue flags. She loved the colour so that for the very last of the season, after everything else would be gone, she cut big broad petals, snipped the edges finely, and made fringed gentians for late October. From the little specks of scraps she made forget-me-nots and blue-eyed grass, while with two small pieces she fashioned two petals to stand up, then was forced to use white for two down · that made such a wonderful little flower she kissed its face twice to put in the life and sweetening, as she named it blue-eyed Mary

When she began on yellow her eyes were gleaming, her lips smiling, her hands flying, because she loved her work so well. She had such stacks and heaps of sunshine she sifted it all over the forest trees for tree bloom, while she heaped it in rough stacks for goldenrod, rolled it in sheets from which to cut petals for daisies and sunflowers, and patted it into big balls like small suns to float on the still

34

HOW THE FLOWERS WERE MADE

water for yellow lilies. She made gloves for the foxes and had gold slippers all ready for the ladies when they came. She shredded gold for the petals of coltsfoot and dandelion, while for the forest floor, for the fields and the mountains, with lavish hand she cut or moulded flowers of gold. She laughed as she made violets from the teeny pieces, then with her fingers she rolled the very last little scraps of all, into sprawling, spidery flowers that she stuck on the bare branches of witch hazel for November.

When she reached the pink cloud heap, it was so very small she was forced to cut carefully; she saw that she would have to make those flowers big and very showy, or there would be so few of them they never would be seen at all among so many others. So for the bushes she made azaleas, laurel bloom, rhododendron, for the trees pink dogwood and peach blossoms, while

35

" She patted it into big balls like small suns for yellow Lilies."

she thought out wild roses for the highways, when they were
made, and bordered the rivers with big blushy mallows
She made moss pink and Bouncing-Bet   From the small
scraps she trailed arbutus among the leaves for the fairy folk.
She mixed white with what was left to make it go farther,
then made apple blossoms for the trees and wild crab bloom,
which she loved so she got it almost too sweet.   She put a
tinge of pink on a turtle head like the white ones she had
made, painted a splash of pink on some of the trillium
petals, and then made big flaring trumpets of white with
broad pink stripes, for the glory of morning.   Then she
made the most beautiful showy party lady slippers, white
with pink toes, because she knew by how lonely she was
that when the ladies came to earth, they would want to
have a party almost right away

There was much more in the purplish heap, so she used
her scissors and fingers deftly in making tears for the red-
bud, the delicate tube of beardtongue, she cut fine moccasins so they would be ready for the Indians, curved the
petals of corncockle, and made purple-flowering raspberry,
like wild roses   She fashioned Queen of the Prairie and
meadow beauty for the fields, while she laughed gaily as a
bird sings when she thought out shooting stars of flowers,
and shook the fringy heads of milkweed bloom, while she
cried for very joy over heather and clover.

When she thought she had finished she saw a heap of a
queer colour she never had seen before   She found that
she had overlooked some dark blue and purplish pink

36

"She made beautiful showy party Lady Slippers, white with pink toes."

lying in a wet place until they had run together and made maroon. She thought from that she would try to make some flowers as peculiar as the colour. When she began to think them out she laughed and laughed over the joke

they would be on her children when they came, and began to hunt to find every single flower she had made for them.

First she made some beautiful lily bells, then she hung them up on the pawpaw branches The next ones were almost like pawpaw bloom, not nearly so funny as she had intended them to be, so she bent their stems and hid them under trillium leaves where her children would have to search a long time to find them, then she named them "wake-robin," so they would be sure to hunt until they did find them For fear they would become discouraged, she cut some narrower petals and set them on the leaves with

38

Lily bells on pawpaw branches.

no stem, so they would be easy to find She cut out
and made a beautiful pulpit, but it was a queer little Jack
she stood in it, to tell all the children who came to the
wood to be gentle and loving with the flowers, and never,
never drag them up by the roots. She was not quite cer-
tain how Jack should look, because she had not yet made
any children; she merely had the thought in the back of
her head that when she got the world all ready, the children surely would come.

She rolled ginger cups, notched the edges and stuck
them at the roots of the plant instead of the top She cut
some of the colour through and through until it resem-
bled raw meat and from it made beefsteak betony She
made a big maroon hood for the heart of the skunk cabbage, and dabbled the outside with splashes of green and
yellow When she went to put in the sweetening the gnats
and mosquitoes bothered her so she rolled them into a little
ball and put some of that inside instead Then she
laughed loudest of all That made her think it would be a
good idea to put some flowers on long stems above the
pitcher plants, so when the insects came to hunt the
sweets they would fall into the pitchers, and help feed the
plants She put hairs inside the pitcher lip so when the
insects tried to climb out they could not. She cut little
ragged strips and made bloom for Adam and Eve orchids,
then used small scraps for clusters of bloom on the
ground-nut vine To the last tiny specks she could find,
she added some yellow, so she would have enough and

39

"She put flowers on long stems above the Pitcher plants, so
when the insects came to hunt the sweets they would fall into

rolled and cut a head of columbine, which was one of the very queerest flowers she had made

All her material was gone She sat there studying her work, snipping grass blades, while she wondered if she had done her very best on everything She thought so intently she snipped too close, cutting her finger badly. When she saw the blood she looked so surprised, because there was no colour like that in all the world. It was redder than the reddest sunset, redder than the red of the rainbow, redder than her lips mirrored in the water Then she began to laugh, while she cut herself again, on purpose.

"That must be the colour of my heart," she cried. "I will fashion flowers from that and have them ready for the lovers when they come." She could not spare much blood, so she stained a piece of moonshine with it, and cut all the flowers from that. It was fine as velvet and red as blood, so she tried her very best to make a wonderful flower She rolled a tube, then she hung three long rather wide petals from it, stuck a very narrow wavy one at each side and finished with a pointed tube sticking up at the top She made dozens of them, she thought them so pretty, she fastened all of them on one stalk, then set it away out in a wet swampy place where it would be very difficult to reach when the children came. She notched narrow straight petals and set them in the deep woods and on the mountainsides where they made a fire for the foxes, which was not easy to find She rolled and fluted tiny tubes for big clustering heads of Oswego tea also, and set

41

them in the swampy places   Then she made a pipe to be ready for the Dutchmen when they came, and dabbled what remained on the brim of a cup for the painters.

All her colours were gone. The spot where she had worked was too lovely for any mortal to describe, while the remainder of the world was plain green like it had been before. She was so tired she lay down and went to sleep right among the Pixie moss and white, blue, and yellow violets. She slept so long the wake-robin leaned over and tickled her nose to rouse her.

She picked up her shears, intending to fly away to bring more colours, when she had the happiest thought in all the world   She thought that instead of wearing herself out to make all the flowers, it would be better to use what she had made for a pattern, and then show each one how to go on making more by itself. "How foolish of me not to have thought of that at first," she said.

She studied for a long, long time, then she began shaping from leaf pulp queer little cups. long cups, round cups, flat cups and pods of every kind you ever saw. Then she thought out and made seed, round seed, flat seed, winged seed, a different kind to fill each cup and pod. She packed all of them tight full, put in lots of sweetening so the bees and butterflies would come to the flowers, then she closed the tiny cups and tucked one away down in the heart of every single bloom, so when the petals fell, it could go on and ripen into good seed to make more flowers. When the seed was ripe some fell down on the

42

ground, some shot far away with a pop, some drifted on the air like thistledown, while some flew on tiny wings with the wind. The seed spread all through the forests, over the fields, climbed the mountains, crept over long stretches of desert sand, and even learned to grow in moss beds on big sheets of ice, away far to the north or south where Santa Claus' reindeers feed.

So that is the way, dear heart, the flowers were made; but if you pull them, you do not let the seeds tucked in their hearts ripen to make more flowers; so after a while all the world will turn plain green again, for Mother Nature says that if we do not take care of the beautiful things she has worked so hard to make for us, she will be so provoked she never, never will make any more. That is true, for when we destroy all of anything, she refuses to ever make more. I couldn't even imagine the world without flowers, Morning Face, could you?

"She cut slender petals for the Daisies."

Come where the hairbell is ringing,
  Where the bluebell its worship call tolls;
Come where the Vireo preaches,
  Where the Hermit his Vesper Song rolls.

LITTLE CHICKENS

"'Oh, what little darlings!'
We *thought* you would cry,
But will we be darlings,
When we're fit to fry?

"From flowers you'll chase us,
With sticks and with stones,
Then you'll soon broil us,
And nibble our bones"

45

"Gene, tell 'bout Bob White and Phoebe Beecher."

BOB WHITE AND PHOEBE BEECHER

Bob White tilled the acres of an Indiana farm,
Phoebe Beecher was his neighbour, full of youthful charm.
As Bob did his farming, Phoebe lingered near:
The birds all helped him woo her, with their notes of
    cheer.

"Spring o' year! Spring o' year!" larks cried overhead
"Wet! Wet! Wet!" the gaudy flickers said
"I'll never finish plowing!" cried the discouraged fellow
"What a pity! What a pity!" wailed a bird with throat of
    yellow.

"Yankey! Yankey! Yank! Yank! Yank!" jeered a nut-
    hatch gray.
"Hire old Sam Peabody! Old Sam Peabody!" Bob
    heard a sparrow say.
"T'check! T'check! T'check!" came the blackbird's pert
    refrain;
"Phoebe'll never have a man who's scared of a little
    rain."

"Cheer up! Cheer up! Cheer up, dearie!" the robins sang
    to Bob;
"Cheer up, dearie! Cheer up, dearie! we'll help you with
    the job."
"Shuck it! Shuck it! Sow it! Sow it!" advised a bird
    of brown,
"Plow it! Plow it! Hoe it! Hoe it! Go it! Hoe it
    down!'"

"Bob! Bob White!" the unseen quail whistled from the
    clover
"I'm plowing," answered Robert, to the saucy mocking
    rover
"Phoebe! Phoebe! Phoebe!" sweet the pewee cried.
"She's coming down the lane," the happy Bob replied.

"Witchery! Witchery! Witchery!" sang a warbler gray
"She has me worse bewitched," said Bob, "every blessed
    day"
"Come to me! Come to me!" intoned a woodland
    thrush.
"Come to me! Come to me!" Bob echoed with a blush.

"I beseech you! I beseech you!" sang a bird of golden
    throat.
"'I beseech you! I beseech you!'" Bob caught up the
    note
"I love, I love, I love you!" the olive thrush repeated;
"'I love, I love you,' Phoebe," the joyful Bob entreated.

48

BOB WHITE AND PHOEBE BEECHER

"Kiss her! Kiss her! Kiss her!" advised the bobolink.
Bob took his advice and kissed her quick as wink.
Chestnut Warbler warbled: "I wish, I wish to see Miss
    Beecher——"
"Preacher! Preacher!" cried the Vireo. "Somebody
    bring a preacher!"

Bob White

ROMEO AND JULIET SQUIRREL

Said Romeo Squirrel: "My heart's in a whirl,
A brand new story I have for your ear.
   Let me squeeze your paw tight,
   While I whisper all night,
How fondly I love you, my Juliet dear!"

GOOD CHILDREN

SOME children of the wood are gentle and good
Like you, when Christmas is near;

BAD CHILDREN

While some squall and fight, from morning 'til night,
Which should be a warning to you, dear.

"Gene, tell 'bout how the Cardinal got his red coat."

HOW THE CARDINAL GOT HIS RED COAT

HE GOT it soon after the great big flood had drowned all the remainder of his family except his mate Their real name was Grosbeak, because they have such big heavy beaks, while their coats were gray, plain, common gray. It was dreadfully lonely with only two Grosbeaks in the whole world, so they hurried to build a sitting-room and started to raise more Grosbeaks.

Theirs was a beautiful sitting-room. Mother Grosbeak was brooding on four bluish-gray eggs, speckled with brown. She was so busy watching the world grow beautiful again, and listening for the first faint movement in her eggs that would tell her the babies were coming, that she seldom became tired; but Father Grosbeak had little to do save to carry her food once in a while or sing and whistle to cheer her up, while he never could keep quiet, especially after having been shut up in the Ark so long, so early one morning he thought he would slip away on a little pleasure trip up the river.

He was flying along, close the water, hopping from bush to bush, chipping about everything he saw. Several

53

times other birds chased him, because he chipped sweet chips to their mates. There were only two of every kind, so all the males were taking the best care ever of their own mates. If Father Grosbeak came hopping up sidewise to any sitting-room and whispered low and sweet, "Dearie, dearie, dearie!" to a little brooding mother, then he would have to fly fast as wind to keep her mate from pulling out a big beakful of his feathers; but he did not care because the very next bird he saw, he would stop and chip the same thing to her.

So he was flying up the river, having a grand time, when on the bank he saw the loveliest sight in the whole world, because there was Mother Nature, when she was young. Her eyes were sky blue, her cheeks were cloud pink, her lips were fire red, her hair was silken sunshine, while her beautiful green dress waved and floated in the wind around her—and there she sat!

She was tired cleaning the flood from everything, for she had to wash away the mud, dry the earth, freshen the trees and bushes and start things growing again. She thought she would sit on the bank to rest awhile, but she had that much to do she could not be entirely idle, so while she rested she was making flowers to brighten the world anew. She had stuck some green stems on the bank to grow while she made the flowers. Then she cut out the prettiest little

54

Cardinal Flower

frmgy blooms you ever saw, dipped them in her pot of red paint, squeezed a drop of honey for the bees into each one of them, also to make them sweet and smelly, then she stuck them on the stalks She called them Cardinal flowers. They were so pretty that when they saw themselves in the water, they grew redder than she made them

She was all so bright and happy; she was humming a soft little murmury song to herself, while she tipped her head to one side to see if she were making those flowers the very prettiest that ever she could, when here came Father Grosbeak, flying beside the river and saw *her !* She was so beautiful she took his breath away

He stopped right there, perched on a limb, flared his crest, fluttered his wings and tried and tried to make her look at him, but she was so interested in making the world fresh again she had no time to pay attention to only one little gray bird, so she went on cutting out the flowers, dipping them into the paint, dropping in the sweetening, and sticking them on their stems. Father Grosbeak tried over and over, but she did not pay any attention, not the slightest He thought she was so beautiful he felt as if he would fly to pieces if he could not make her notice him soon, so he leaned far toward her, flared his crest, spread and fluttered his wings, while he called tender and loving as ever he could· "Girlie, girlie, girlie!"

Mother Nature never looked up, but he was watching her very close, so he noticed her hands moved a little slower; then he hopped closer, spread his wings wider, and called a little lovinger: "Dearie, dearie, dearie!"

Mother Nature stopped short, looked straight at him; then she smiled, and when she smiled, why then she was beautifuler than anything else in the whole world She made Father Grosbeak feel so wild in his head, he hopped right close to her, rocking and fluttering, his feathers quivered, his eyes gleamed, while he begged and pled all so sweet and loving· "Come here! Come here! Come here!"

Mother Nature sat still, holding a flower she had just dipped into the red paint, trying to pretend she did not care; but she did. She was pleased as could be. She was so pleased she had to listen, because every one had been so busy cleaning up after the flood, and getting ready to live on the ground again, they had not had time yet to go out and live with her, to make up songs praising her beauty, to write stories and poems about her, to paint pictures of her face, and to tell her over and over how they loved her; so what Father Grosbeak told her sounded so new, and so good she could not help listening. She became so flustrated she never saw a big black and green striped butterfly having long trailers, that had alighted in her lap and was nosing around her honey pot Her hand shook so she let a drop of red paint fall right on one of his back wings a little above the trailer

"I thought I was finished, Mother," he said to her.

She said "You are, Ajax. I made you handsome as ever I knew how"

HOW THE CARDINAL GOT HIS RED COAT

"Then why did you put that red on my wing?" he asked.

And she said: "Land of love, Ajax! If there is red on you my hand shook so I spilled it."

"Take it off!" cried Ajax.

"I can't!" said Mother Nature. "That paint is indelible; it won't ever come off."

"Then what will I do?" asked Ajax. "I don't want one red spot on me."

So Mother Nature laughed as she said: "Sit over there on that flower, son, raise your wings above your back, and hold them together tight, so half that paint will stick to your other wing. Then spread them and sit in the sun until they dry, and you will be two little specks better looking than you were before; then you fly straight away, because I have no time to bother with butterflies around my honey right now."

She smiled again at Father Grosbeak. He went so crazy he came flying full tilt and perching in her lap he sang: "So dear! So dear! So dear!"

Mother Nature stirred softly and bent over him so lovingly, but no

57

"Raise your wings and hold them together tight."

one will ever know just what she was going to say, because there came Mother Grosbeak, tired with brooding all night, while she had no bath, and no early worm. She saw him sitting in Mother Nature's lap, singing the song Mother Grosbeak loved best so she felt very cross She cried to him "Chook! Chook! Why don't you come home and brood until I take my bath and find my breakfast?"

Father Grosbeak drew his gray coat close around him and sat there afraid to move, while Mother Nature and Mother Grosbeak stared at each other, then quick as light, Mother Nature caught Father Grosbeak and stuck him splash! into her red paint pot. Then she held him there until every feather on him was soaked good and red. She held him down, and held him, until he choked and choked so that he *turned black in the face* Then she lifted him up, brushed away the clouds and let the hot sun shine on him to dry him quick.

When he was dry she gave him a push and said "There! You want to make love so badly, I'll just change your gray coat to love's own colour, so each and every bird in the woods will know you as far as they can see you."

Then she jumped up and went sailing away across the river, angry as she could be, while Father Grosbeak sat shaking his head to get the red paint from his mouth, as he turned redder and redder every minute.

Mother Grosbeak cried "Chook! Chook! My dear, you are ruined." Then she began to tell him it was all her fault, while she worked to rub the paint off with her beak,

58

"Get into the water and bathe "

feet and wings until she became *tinged* with red herself.
Father Grosbeak saw what she was doing, so he chipped:
"Look out! You will get it all over you!"

She hurried to the river to bathe, soak and try to wash
away the red; but she did not know that Mother Nature's
paint was indelible so it would never come off. She tried
to get it off, then she flew to Father Grosbeak, seized him
by the wing, pulled him to the water and started to push
him in. He perched on a twig and leaned to wash his

59

mouth, when he saw his red coat. He was so surprised he almost fell into the water. He forgot all about washing his mouth and began to fluff his red feathers, flirt his tail and chip and chatter, he was so delighted

Mother Grosbeak thought he had gone crazy as a Loon. She screamed at him: "Chook! Chook! Get into the water and bathe the dreadful stuff away, quickly!"

Father Grosbeak cried "Chip! Chip!" But he sailed to the top twig of the highest tree he could see and spread his wings to dry the colour faster, he was so proud of his new coat, while he whistled and cried to every bird passing: "See here! See here!"

Mother Grosbeak was so provoked at him she rubbed and worked to get the tinge of red she could see on herself, off. She scoured her beak on the stones and tried to bite the colour from her wings and toes, but she could not change it back to gray again; so at last she thought about her sitting-room and her eggs becoming chilled, then she hurried back home

After a long time Father Grosbeak went to her still chipping proudly about his new coat; but when he saw how badly she felt he promised sure that he never, never again would sing her songs to any other birds, and he never has; but always since he has been black in the face and his coat has been red, so his name that belongs to his family alone has been changed to Cardinal.

THE BLUE TURTLE

WAY down on the bay of Funday
On a blue and misty Monday,
In a bed of creeping myrtle,
Hatched a scrumptious little turtle.
'Cause the weather and flowers were blue,
He always felt that colour, too.

61

"Gene, tell me what the Horned Owl says"

HORNED OWL

"When the moonlight floods the swampland,
  When the bittern's wailing croak,
    And the wildcat's scream of anger
  Clog the heart of forest folk,
    I search tall trees for frightened crows,
  Hunt ducks 'neath sedges, hares at play,
    Then I set late travellers trembling,
  By demanding until break of day:

"'Who, who, huh, whoo, who waugh?
    Don't I make cold shivers run?
  Who, huh, hoo, whoo? I'd question all day,
    If my eyes could bear the sun '"

"And tell me 'bout the Barn Owl."

THE BARN OWL

'WHEN weary work horses are stabled,
  When sleeping lie cattle and sheep,
    When the rat's tooth grates in the silence,
  From my dark, warm tree I creep;
    I fly to white doves on the rafters,
  To chickens on the stalls below,
  Make my feast upon the choicest,
    Then awaken you jeering as I go.

"'Hoo, hoo, hoo, hoot! Hoo, hoo, hoo, hoot!
  Read the story in feathers white,
  To-whit, to-hoot! Hoo, hoo, hoo, hoot!
  I'll call again to-morrow night '"

" Screech Owl, too!"

THE SCREECH OWL

"When the fireflies light their lanterns,
  When the locusts rasp their files,
    And the whip-poor-will's sad wailing
  Fills the dusky forest aisles;
    I come from my daytime hiding,
  Catch small sleeping birds to eat,
    Then I cock one ear, and I wink one eye
  As I give you this musical treat:

"'It's, Hoo, hoo, hoo, hoo!   Hoo, hoo, hoo, hoo!
    Don't you wish you had me in reach?
  Hoo, hoo, hoo, hoo!   Hoo, hoo, hoo, hoo!
    Say, *how* do you like my screech?'"

A KISS

SAID tulip one, to tulip two:
"There's great joy we should not miss.
Bend your tulips to my tulips,
And that will be a kiss."

Cynthia Samia

"She met her mate."

MISS CYNTHIA SAMIA

Cynthia Samia
Left her neat
Warm cocoon,
And went to try life,
By the light
Of the moon.
She met her mate
And laid her eggs,
That same night.
Alas! then
Poor Cynthia
Faded from sight.

69

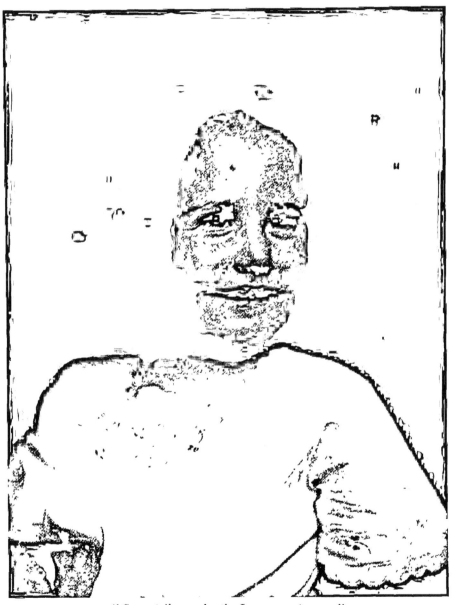

"Gene, tell me why the Loons went crazy."

WHY THE LOONS WENT CRAZY

It was at the time of the great big flood-water, when it rained and it rained. It rained until the water came up, and came up, until it was the very highest ever Before it got the highest ever a man named Noah thought it was going to cover the whole earth, so he built a boat big enough for his family, and for one pair of every kind of bird and animal there was in the world

When they came to putting the birds in the boat they caught the water birds first, because the longer it rained, the more water they would have to swim away in, while the less land the others would have to hide on After they thought they had every kind, some one discovered they had no Loons, so they started out to get a pair, but those birds liked the water so well they would not leave it After they had hunted all around the shore Mr. Noah and his sons went home discouraged saying 'Verily, we fail to catch those diving, swimming water birds "

Then Mrs. Noah said. "They are so beholden to water, I fear thou must go in thy fishing boat and use nets "

So Mr. Noah and his sons went in their small boat,

71

tangled a pair of loons in the nets and fished them from
the water they loved so well   Then they put them in a
small dark place, with *sand* under their feet and only a
little, teeny bit of water to *drink,* none to splash their feet
in, or to bathe in, or to hunt things to eat in, just a little
to drink

Mother Loon was so angry she beat her head, flapped
her wings and screamed, just screamed, and screamed,
until she almost killed herself, but it did no good, because
there were all the tree birds, the bush birds, the land and
the water birds coming into the boat, and all the land and
water animals; so at the same time the big Eagles and
Hawks were screaming louder than any Loon ever could,
but no one could hear even them, because the Lions were
roaring, "Arraugh, arraugh, arraugh!'" while the Tigers
were screaming, "Erough, erough, erough," and the Sea
Lions bellowed, "Ough, ough, ough."   All the little birds
were crying, chipping and chattering about being taken
from the trees, land, and water, so while Mother Loon
screamed as loud as ever she could, she simply *could not*
scream louder than all the others put together

Old Father Loon screamed too, as loud as ever he could,
but when no one paid any attention Mother Loon was so
distracted she flew at that little bit of water and *spilled* it.
Then she tried to slap her feet and sousle her head in it,
but she got all dirty in the sand, while she had no water
to wash herself clean   When Old Father Loon wanted
to slap *his* feet and sousle *his* head, there was no water at

72

all, so he went into the darkest corner and cried and cried. That made Mother Loon feel so badly, she flew at the walls and beat them with her *head* and wings until she was all bloody, quite bleeding bloody; while the rain it came down, and came down on the boat, so that the water went washing by, and washing by, all around them until they could *hear it, just every minute they could hear it.*

Old Mother Loon would scarcely eat a bite, because she wanted *wet* things, and *green* things, and *wormy* things, while Father Loon wanted exactly what she did.

"Wet things, and green things, and wormy things."

MORNING FACE

Every morning they had so little water, Mother Loon barely got her bill and feet wet before it was gone, all gone until the next sun-up, so her bill and tongue turned *all yellow*, while her legs and feet grew yellow, and the skin between her toes *dried up;* then her crop drew *away* inside and her feathers *pulled* and *stuck*, so that she was perfectly *miserable*.

Old Father Loon, he was more miserable than she was, because he was so polite he always let the ladies eat and drink first, so Mother Loon took almost all of the little bit of water. He lay down on the sand and *dried up*, until he was only bones and feathers, because he needed more water so badly Mother Loon, after she had screamed and fussed until she could not make another sound, why then she lay down and dried up too, while all the time the rain poured down close above them, and the water *gurgled* and *sousled*, and *splashed* right beside them.

Mother and Father Loon thought they would surely *die;* they grew so very miserable they beat their heads and tried to dive right through the boat bottom, because they were burning up so, while *everywhere* the water was splashing, except where they were.

Then one sun-up, why the rain it stopped The water went down and went down until the trees and then the land stuck up through, then the boat settled firmly on a mountain. As soon as there was land enough uncovered Mr Noah let all and everything come from the

74

boat and go away. They were tickled almost to death
to get back to the land and water, because no wild thing
likes being shut up in a cage and fed by men.

When everything had come out and gone away, Mr.
Noah said to Mrs. Noah: "Has everything come forth?"
She answered: "I did not see the Loons They rebelled
worst of all. Perhaps thou wilt be forced to carry them
out." So Mr. Noah went into the boat to the Loons'
cage and there they lay so far gone they did not know
they were alone, he picked them up by the wings, carried
them out and set them beside the water They just lay
there, because they were so dried up they did not even
know water when they saw it. Then old Mother Loon,
she thought *maybe* it was water, so she reached out and
slapped one foot, soft and easy, and it splashed like water.
Then old Father Loon reached out and slapped one foot,
the same as she did, and it *did* splash like water Then
old Mother Loon slapped the other foot, and it seemed
like water, so Father Loon slapped with his other foot,
real hard, and the splash made him *sure* it was water.
Then Mother Loon, going first, like she always did, just
reached over and stuck her head into it, sousing it around
till it felt so *wet*, so *cool* and so *good*, she almost *knew* it
had to be water She looked at Father Loon so surprised
like, then she sat back on her tail and began to laugh and
to cry at the same time.

Then right after her Father Loon sousled his head, until
it felt so wet and fine, he sat back on his tail and laughed

and cried harder than she did. They both plunged into that water, *splash !* to bathe their skins, soak their feet, dip their heads, wet their feathers, to drink and *drink,* and gobble a fat juicy worm, yes and they got some green weeds with it, so they just *knew* it *had* to be *real, for sure enough water* They were so glad they just *cried,* and *laughed* and *screamed* until they went clear *crazy* over that water. Then they swam far away from everything, so no man would ever catch them *again;* but every night Mr. and Mrs. Noah and their family could hear them laughing and screaming, quite as crazy as they were when they swam away.

So Mr Noah said to Mrs Noah· "Didst thou ever behold anything so crazy as those Loons?"

Mrs. Noah answered· "Verily, I never, never did! And as they are the only pair left to multiply and replenish the earth, I fear after this all the loons will be crazy "

So they always have been.

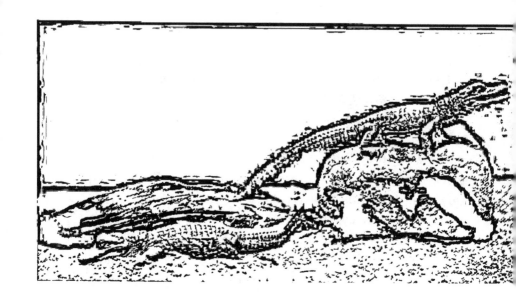

JOHN AND JANE ALLIGATOR

Down in the land of the Cassowary,
Elephant, Lion and Dromedary,
Close our only nice warm equator,
Lived little John and Jane Alligator.

Jane slept all day, stretched out on the sand,
John was more wakeful, toothful, and bland.
Here is the safest place they can meet you;
At the equator, they surely would eat you

"GENE, DO SING-SONG 'BOUT THE FLOWERS"

MISS ROSE MARY lost her breath,
Turned up her toes and died an awful death,
'Cos Skunk Cabbage stuck up his head,
Close beside her in the Orchid bed.

Creeping Charlie danced hop-scotch,
When he lost Solomon's Seal with his watch.
Nimble Kate tossed back her locks,
And said: "Tell your time by the Four o'clocks."

Pussy Willow went to the Milkweed bed,
To see that her kittens were properly fed.
They were scared coming home in the dark,
Because the mean old Dog Wood bark.

"Touch-me-not!" Blue-eyed Mary said,
When Sweet William tried to turn her head.
He offered Blue Bonnets and Queen Anne's Lace,
If she'd let him kiss her lovely face.

Queen of the Prairie ruling all alone,
Asked Meadow Beauty to share her throne.
Midsummer Men riding Side-saddle flower,
Came to drink Painter's Cup in Virgin's Bower.

78

Fox Fire

Fox Fire started a flame in the woods,
Burned Black-eyed Susan's household goods.
She couldn't replace them for years and years,
    And that was what caused so many Job's Tears.

79

MORNING FACE

Jack-in-the-Pulpit, smoking Indian Pipe,
Asked Joe Pye when June Berries were ripe.
Joe laughed at him saying. "I can't remember
  That I ever ate May Apples in December."

Monkey Flower played such a naughty trick,
He made his Mother's Heart almost sick.
Marigold said "I wonder if you can't
  Change his ways with Obedient Plant."

Herb St. Barbara was so very good,
She wanted Herb Robert to wear Monk's Hood.
He said "Quaker Bonnets better suit me,
  With Moccasins, Honey Balls and Oswego Tea."

Bouncing Bet went to the Fair,
To buy Gipsy Combs for her Maiden Hair,
Lady's Thimble, Gold Slippers and Tresses,
  Jewel Flowers, Ear Drops, and Everlasting dresses.

St. Andrew's Cross was heavy to bear,
When he had Dutchman's Breeches to wear.
He said he looked like the Wandering Jew,
  All dressed up in Whip-poor-Will's Shoe.

Ox-eye winked at Adam and Eve
Saying. "If they were parted they'd surely grieve.
I'll send them Pitcher Plant and Allspice hot,
  So they will Forget-me-not!"

THE QUEER RAIN

"I THINK it is very queer
But really, it is raining drops,
About as big as half a tear."

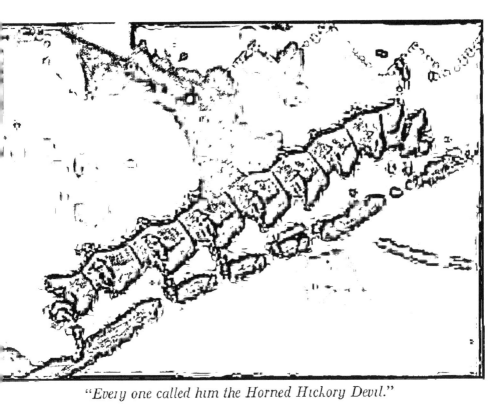

"Every one called him the Horned Hickory Devil."

THE PATHETIC CATERPILLAR

A FLOCK of caterpillars blue and stickery,
Lived upon my Dutch Cape hickory,
Over the beefsteak betony bed,
Among flowers yellow, maroon and red
They had ten tan horns with tips of black,
And sharp little stickers on the back.

One, of a beauteous blue-green colour,
Was fat as any fresh fried cruller.
He looked so fierce as on leaves he'd revel,
Every one called him the Horned Hickory Devil.

He ate, and ate, with all his might,
He ate every hickory leaf in sight.
He ate and ate, oh grievous sin!
He ate, until he burst his skin.
He burst his skin, and never cried,
'Cause he knew he'd a bigger skin inside.
So when he'd burst, with resounding pop,
He'd eat again, like he couldn't stop

MORNING FACE

All day he ate, the plump blue sinner,
As much as you'd eat for Thanksgiving dinner;
And every night, while you slept sweet,
He stayed awake, to eat and eat.
He ate until he looked greedy and mean,
He ate until his blood turned green,
He ate till he lost every skin he had,
Should he burst again, 'twould be very sad.

When he was blue, as the bluest chicory,
And the biggest 'pillar on the hickory,
A wicked green wasp observed his size,
And paused to watch him gourmandize
The wasp licked his chops, then with his six feet,
Started where the 'pillar continued to eat.
He watched him trimming leaves like a bevel,
Then said· "I believe I'll go to the Devil."

He bit a big hole in the 'pillar's blue side,
So the greedy Horned Devil speedily died
And when, with a loud report, he burst,
The wasp drank all his green blood he durst
Then he cried to every wasp flying that way:
"Stop, friend, you are asked to my banquet, to-day.

The 'pillar's blue skin hung limp across a leaf,
While the rest of his family ate on in grief.
The moral is plain· Don't eat too energetic,
Or your end, like the 'pillar's, may be pathetic,

THE HICKORY MOTH

For he missed being this Moth, because of his greed,
Which is a remarkably sad thing, indeed!

"At the slipper I'll meet you nightly."

"Katydid."

KATYDID AND GALLINIPPER

ONCE a saucy Gallinipper,
Mooning on a lady-slipper,
Flipped Miss Katydid, with his flipper,
Till she flew to the Big Dipper.

Katy sat there on the handle,
Scratched a match upon her sandal,
With it lighted up her candle
To watch Gallinipper dandle.

Cried she in a voice quite mocking:
"Gallinipper, this is shocking!
You have set my heart to rocking,
Now to you, my door I'm locking."

Pled the Gallinipper, purry:
"Katy dear, I'm in a flurry.
Don't condemn me in a hurry!
You will cause my death of worry."

Answered Katy: "Ask politely,
Prove you're feeling quite contritely,
At the slipper I'll meet you nightly,
When the moon is shining whitely."

"Gene, tell me 'bout the Screech Owl babies."

SCREECH OWL BABIES

THEY just left home in the big gray beech,
And they're called Screech Owls, because they screech

Little top owl was the first from his shell,
His parents always fed him very well.
He had sharp claws and eyes open wide,
So he was his mother's nightly pride.

Next below him comes his little brother,
Also the special joy of his mother.
His beak is sharp and keen is his eye,
He can raise your hair with his shrill cry

Then comes little sister, neat and nice,
Instead of candy she likes whole mice
A better Screech Owl never was seen,
She doesn't act a teeny bit mean

Last is the baby, as you can see,
The pet and pride of the fam-i-lee,
She eats every bat that comes in reach,
And gracious me, you should hear her screech!

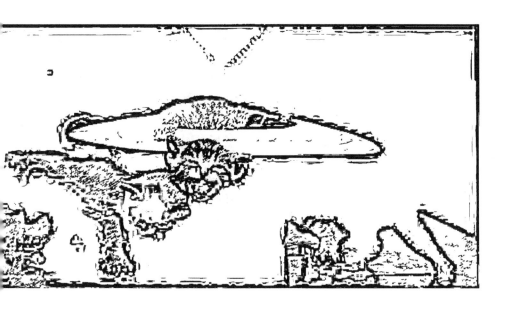

THE UNHAPPY CATS

WE ARE most unhappy cats,
We don't like Mexican hats,
We don't want our pictures taken,
We feel terribly forsaken,
Want mammy and our nest in the mow,
Meow! Meow! Meow! Meow!

90

THE SNOW BOYS

THE courting owls wake the Snow Boys white,
  When the first cold bee is humming.
So they lift pale faces to the light,
  To tell us that joy is coming.

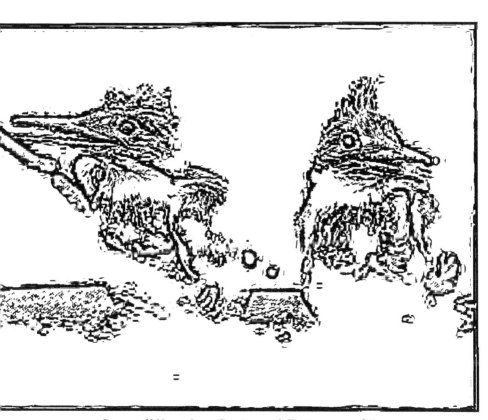

"*Gene, tell 'bout how Spotty and Dotty quarrel.*"

"Minny Kingfisher."

HOW DOTTY AND SPOTTY KINGFISHER QUARREL

"Urrrrrrrr! Bless my bones!" rattled Father Billy Kingfisher, as he flew homeward from the river. He hurried down Paradise Alley, crossed the gravel pit and sailed over the frog-pond lying below his front door, where he alighted in haste, crying: "Whatever is all this noise about?"

"Urrrrr, Billy!" replied Mother Minny, leaving their sitting-room and hurrying to meet him at the door of the long hall. "The twins persist in quarreling."

"How amazing!" exclaimed Billy. "When that boy-animal tore up our cradle and broke five of our eggs with a stick, I was not utterly desolate. We could mend the cradle, have omelet for breakfast, while it did seem that twins would be a rest, after the families for which we have been providing in the past. But I never was more mis-

93

taken. This pair has the appetites of the seven we expected, while the more they eat, the faster they grow and the worse they behave. The boy will come again if they are not quiet."

"I do the best I can," explained Minny. "They are so full of life, while they are the cunningest nestlings we ever have had."

"If you will remember you say that every migration," said Billy. "I suppose these are exactly like the others. You notice them more because you have time to look at them. How are they feathering?"

"Finely! Scarcely a pin shows in their suits. Having only the pair, I fear we have almost stuffed them, and if there is one thing I detest above all others, it is a stuffed bird——'

"Urrrrrrrr!" laughed Billy.

"You sound like a braying donkey," said Mother Minny, angrily. "What is the matter?"

"How you must feel about me!" laughed Billy. "I always come home stuffed, and go away empty."

"Urrr!' giggled Minny "So you do! But I was telling you about our blessed babies. Of course their beaks and eyes will grow larger, their crests will flare higher, yet they surpass any youngsters I ever have seen right now "

"Nothing new," interrupted Billy.

"Have you really noticed the breadth and whiteness of their collars?" asked Minny. "Have you seen that Spotty's breastband is blue as his back, while Dotty's is

94

brown as Mr. Thrush. Their coats are sky blue, while his vest and her apron are lily white?"

"So they are," said Father Billy.

"We couldn't have named them more appropriately," continued Minny. "Every mark on Spotty is a small irregular spot, while on ~~Minny~~ Dotty it is a perfectly round dot. I am so glad we didn't name them for ourselves. I am tired of looking at your big bill and then calling you Billy, and of having you call me Minny while I eat fish. And if I do mention it myself, I keep them clean. No birds can chatter that we are dirty, even living in a dug-out!"

"Hear Mummy brag about me?" inquired Spotty, in the cradle back in the sitting-room.

"It is about me 'ist as much!" retorted Dotty indignantly.

"No such thing!" rattled Spotty. "My last lunch I had a minnow and a blackberry, so the berry juice made the fishbones all black; then when I guggil-tated they went against you and soiled your collar dref-fully. You are not a clean bird!"

"I am too!" answered

95

"I shall ask politest, so she will give it to me."

MORNING FACE

Dotty, struggling to twist her head so that she could see her neck. "Mummy knows I am clean— 'sides it's reguggiltated, anyway!"

"I am going to have the next fish!" announced Spotty. "I shall sit straighter, stick my bangs higher and act cuter than you, so Mummy will give it to me."

"I'll ask politest, so she will give it to me," retorted Dotty. "You are always thinking about your looks."

"I am not!" rattled Spotty, growing angry. "'Always' means all the time. What I am thinking right now is,—that when Mummy goes fishing again I shall drive you to the front door and push you down into Mr. Frog's pond."

"Urrr, Spotty!" rattled Dotty, reproachfully.

"I shall!" insisted Spotty, stoutly. "And when you light ker-splash! the old cross Mummy Frog will croak: 'Shitepokes! What kind of new baby has rained down to me? I shall be compelled to make this creature all over before it can live with us. It doesn't look a particle like a Frog anywhere, except its eyes.' Then she will seize you and unpin every feather on you. She will strip you all bare naked. The water will be so cold you will 'ist shiver and rattle dreffully."

"Urrrrrrrrrr, Spotty!" quavered Dotty.

Spotty continued remorselessly: "Then your new Frog Mummy will croak: 'No one ever heard of a Frog having a long beak.

"I shall drive you to the front door and push you down into Mr. Frog's Pond."

96

That must come off!' Then she will take you to a very
rough stone and rub your bill against it, and rub and rub
It will hurt you worse than all the fishbones that ever
scratched you, made into one big bone, making one big
scratch, but she won't ever care   She'll 'ist rub and rub,
'nen you'll have a great big wide-open Frog mouth."

"I won't!" rattled Dotty

"Oh yes you will!' teased Spotty.   "And then she'll
croak· 'My sun and my song! Was there ever 'nother
such Frog? Here it is with forelegs three times too long
and hindlegs three times too short' 'Nen she'll begin
pushing your wings right back inside you.   She'll push,
and push, and push, till she makes little funny short Frog
forelegs from them, so you'll never, never get to fly
You'll 'ist rattle, and rattle with the dreffle hurt of it,
while I'll look down and laugh and ask you: 'Now, don't
you wish you hadn't 'bused me?'"

"I haven't 'bused you, Spotty!" cried Dotty, her big
eyes popping with fear as she backed against the farthest
wall of the sitting-room

"You have!" insisted Spotty   "'Nen she'll begin on
your legs.   She'll pull, and pull, while you will rattle
and rattle.   Our Mummy will hear you and she will cry:
'Good for such a bad bird!' Your new Frog Mummy
will keep right on pulling, until she pulls your little bits
of short Kingfisher legs out into great long Frog legs
'Nen when you want to go anywhere you'll have to
hop along on the ground, but you can always look up and

97

see *me* flying around among the tree tops! Every time
you stick your head above the water to get your breath,
a boy-animal will try to hit it with a stone, so he can tear
off your legs and take them home to fry for his supper."

Dotty shivered in silent terror

"'Nen," continued Spotty, pleased with his success,
"she'll take a great big stone and beat you until your back
is all greenery-yellow, and she'll make you lie on the bank
in the sun, until it burns your tummy all yellery-green.
Then she'll throw you into awful cold water and make you
sit and sing 'Purt! Purt! Purt!' all the whole night
long; but you'll know I'm sound asleep in our cradle
tucked safe and warm against Mummy's breast."

"Urrrrr, Spotty!" wailed Dotty.

"And then," Spotty finished with a flourish, "boy-
animals will catch you in a net, sticked 'way down in the
water where you can't ever hide from it. They will run
a big sharp hook under your chin up through your mouth
and out of your nose, and drop you in the river for fish
bait You'll see a great big black catfish, long as our hall,
and all slickery black and yellow, having big sharp horns,
coming straight at you, and he'll see you and stop He'll
think · 'How nice and fat that Frog is! B'lieve I'll eat him!'
'Nen that catfish will bite you dreffully and swallow you
very slow, like Mummy sees them at the river every day.
She'll see it eat you, but she won't ever care."

Dotty rattled in anguish.

"Spotty! Dotty!" Mother Minny rattled "You'll

have that boy-animal after us again. If you don't stop
I'll put both of you in your cradle and sit on you until
you half smother. Spotty, I believe you are teasing again.
Kiss your dear little nest-mate on the spot!"

"Which spot?" questioned Spotty.

"The nice little one on her cheek."

So Spotty gave Dotty a little kiss, without a bit of love
in it and then they snuggled into the beautiful cradle their
mother had made them from the fishbones she regurgi-
tated while she was brooding over them. But Dotty
looked steadily at Spotty with big reproachful eyes, until
he began to squirm. At last she told him, very softly: "I
want you to be a beautiful bird that can fly to the river
and go fishing. I wouldn't ever push you into the water
to be made into a old croaky Frog."

"Dotty, I was 'ist p'tendin'," said Spotty. "I ain't
going to push you, really!"

"Then," offered Dotty, "you may sleep with your
bill across my neck."

Father Billy Kingfisher

"Babes of the Woods, I am forced to relate,
Must eat what their mothers re-gur-gi-tate."

BABES O' THE WOODS

You have a cariole, dainty and white,
With a silken comfort tucked close at night.
Babes of the Woods have a snug little nest,
And the feather cover on mother's breast.

You have a fork for your nicely cooked food,
And I hope you are never greedy or rude.
Babes of the Woods, I am forced to relate,
Must eat what their mothers re-gur-gi-tate.

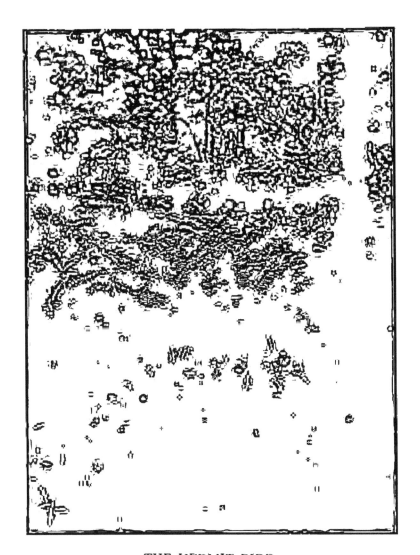

THE HERMIT BIRD

In wooded tangle where vibrant air,
   With wing of down and gauze is stirred,
A miracle of pain-sweet sound burst forth,
   And lo, the voice of the Hermit Bird!

SAMMY AND SUSY SHRIKE

Sammy Shrike and Susy Shrike,
They went and fought, oh my!
Till their mother sent them both to bed
Each wearing a black eye.

When I go to play with Gene,
Munner always starts me clean.

ROMPERS

WHEN I am munner's little girl,
Every hair's brushed in a curl
I wear 'broidery an' ruffley lace,
You never saw a cleaner face;
Socks an' sashes an' butterfly bows.
I'm all sweet smelly, like a rose

When I go to play with Gene,
Munner always starts me clean,
But she says just omperns are right,
'Cos I'm sure to come back a sight.
But I have the mostest fun,
Dressed so I can climb and run.

Gene can't bother with dry goods,
When we plant flowers in her woods.
We can't fuss with ribbon and trills, .
When we go to wild strawberry hills
We can drink from leaves of pawpaw,
But such spilly business you never saw

We catch speckly fish in the brook,
With our hands 'stead of a hook.
We string raspberries on a straw,
And gather apples of scarlet haw
When I go home munner says. "It's true,
When you play with Gene, just 'omperns' will do."

"We're the real cuckoo clock"

THE CUCKOO CLOCK

P'RAPS 'twill give your nerves a shock,
But we're the *real* Cuckoo Clock.
Our first· "Cuck-ooh!" that's your warning,
To jump from bed early in the morning.
"Cuck-ooh!" at noon, plow-boy or tinner,
Hurries straight home to eat his dinner.
"Cuck-ooh!" again, sure as you're alive!
Calls you to supper, at half-past five.
When we cry "Cuck-ooh!" last time at night,
Jump into bed and shut your eyes tight
Any other time we call "Cuck-ooh" plain,
That's a sure sign it's going to rain

"Twenty-seven small ducks, each cutting an antic,
Ran straight to that puddle, which drove the hen frantic."

THE BAD LITTLE DUCKS

TWENTY-SEVEN small quackers, all yellow and fluffy,
Lived with their hen mother in a coop that was stuffy
Unheeding her warnings they would run far away,
So she clucked and she scolded the whole livelong day.

She told them to eat bugs, and scratch for a living,
But she should have saved the advice she was giving
You can see very plainly no one had taught her,
A duck can't be kept from a puddle of water

So when thunder rolled, like a great big bass drum,
She spread her wings widely and begged them to come;
But the harder it rained the worse they amazed her.
Such things as they did completely crazed her

They ran through the rain, and gobbled in feeding,
They quacked and they quarreled as if they'd no breeding
The more the hen scolded the wetter they got,
Soon a big puddle formed, right in the barn lot.

Twenty-seven small ducks, each cutting an antic,
Ran straight to that puddle, which drove the hen frantic.
They swam and they dived, they drank and they gobbled,
While poor Mother Orpington jumped 'till she wobbled.

MORNING FACE

One small yellow duck gulped a nice fat snail,
Of little brown duck she could see only the tail
The other young rascals all ate, drank and paddled,
Until the old settin' hen went entirely addled.

She was so flustered she 'most died of fright,
For they stayed in that puddle until it was night.
Then they came waddling back, each little sinner,
With a tummy quite full of his favourite dinner

And if you'll believe me, after acting so badly,
After scaring and grieving their mother so sadly,
She spread her yellow wings and clucked them to rest,
All the heads she could cover against her warm breast

MORNING GLORY MUSIC

We found these glories among
    the corn,
    On a crisp, glowing Septem-
    ber morn.
Seeds the song birds had im-
    planted there,
    Flaunted their gay trumpets
    everywhere;
While many a Fairy, in robe of
    lace,
    To make glad music for
    Morning Face,
Came gaily dancing over the
    corn,
    Each blowing a Morning
    Glory horn.

111

"Roadside redbird courting sang: 'Good Cheer! Good Cheer!'"

RUBEN AND THE REDBIRD

MARCH

"GOOD CHEER!"

Ruben went to see his sweetheart, March day cool and
  clear,

Roadside redbird courting sang "Good Cheer! Good
  Cheer!"

On the way they met their Quaker maidens gray,

All their hearts were singing, "Good cheer," all that day.

Chorus:

"Good cheer!" little sweethearts, "Good cheer," all the
  day,

Happy hearts and faces make a sunnier way.

Never time for pining or an hour that's drear,

While the heart is singing. "Cheer! Good Cheer! Good
  Cheer!"

APRIL

"Wet year!"

Once in changeful April, Ruben's steps lagged slow.

"Wet year!" sang the redbird, sweetheart's tears o'er-
  flow

Ruben's heart was melted, he was filled with grief,

"Wet year!" sang the redbird, for his heart's relief.

Chorus:

"Wet year!" little sweethearts, life is sometimes pain,

Hearts must stoutly battle when the day brings rain,

Sunshine in the morning, evening may be drear,

Redbird will be singing. "Year! Wet year! Wet year!"

MAY

"Come here!"

Then on blithesome Mayday, Ruben's arms spread wide,
"Come here!" coaxed the redbird, "come and be his
 bride!
Come for joy or sorrow! Come for health or pain,
Come here! Come here, sweetheart, never part again!"

Chorus

"Come here, little sweetheart, come to love and life,
Come to him who waits you, be his happy wife,
Come on sunny Mayday, banish Autumn gloom,
Come here, come here, sweetheart, all the world's in
 bloom."

JUNE

"So dear!"

"So dear!" sang the redbird, every day in June,
"So dear," sang glad Ruben, all the world in tune.
In the thicket redbird sang in trembling fear,
In a cottage Ruben, "Dear, so dear! So dear!"

Chorus·

"So dear," little sweethearts, life is joyful pain,
"So dear," in the sunshine, "So dear," in the rain,
"So dear," in the evening, or the morning clear,
"So dear," little sweethearts, always "Dear! So dear!"

*"In the thicket redbird sang in trembling fear,
In a cottage Ruben: 'Dear!   So dear, So dear!'"*

MORNING FACE

"See here!"

"See here!" sang the redbird, wild in July glee,

"See here!" shouted Ruben, "you're ahead of me!

But next year I'll join you in a song of cheer,

When my nestling's cradled, I'll sing· "Here! See
here!"

Chorus·

"See here!" little sweethearts, life is full and wide,

Nestlings winging, toddling footsteps, ever at your side,

"See here," little mothers, hearts of loving fear,

"See here," happy fathers, "Here! See here! See
here!"

FATHER PIGEON

FATHER pigeon loves his wife,
  For kisses he hourly begs;
Once he crowded up so close,
  He pushed her off her eggs.

117

"*They carefully built their sitting-room.*"

THE FIRST CONCERT

AFTER the flood Wood Robin with his mate Bell chose
a damp, cool location beside the water, where pink mallows flowered and soft winds spiced with wine-coloured
pawpaw bloom waved the fringy willows Here, among
the wild grape that clambered over a giant elm tree,
they carefully built their sitting-room

The very next day they heard a voice they recognized
and Wood started to find exactly where it came from. He
soon discovered that his cousin and only rival Hermit
Thrush and his mate the Swamp Angel were building
their sitting-room across the little bay. They were work-
ing on a home in a tangle of button bushes, above which
giant forest trees shut out most of the light, and beneath
tall fern fronds and feathery marsh grasses waved over
leaf-lined pools whose purple surfaces were broken by
ragged patches of silver, where the light fell strongest and
sentinel torches of fox fire flamed at the very edge of the
water.

Wood went home appearing thoughtful

"What is the trouble?" inquired Bell, as she tucked a
piece of grape bark into the cradle lining

119

"Cousin Hermit has settled in the button bushes across the bay."

"Lee! Lee!" exclaimed Bell. "I am delighted. With only one pair living of every family on earth, company is so scarce, we certainly are unusually blest in having a near relative so close."

"If the musical reputation of the family depended on you, perhaps you would not be so pleased "

"Why not?"

"Lee! Lee! If you would take more interest in me and less in that cradle, you would understand."

"You forget, Wood, that on the outcome of this cradle rests the future of our family If we do not produce a brood before anything happens to either of us, Hermit is left undisputedly the Prince of Song."

"Lee! Lee! I had forgotten that. But he is not the Prince of Song now, is he? Are not my notes more musical than his?"

"Of course I think so, but you may believe the Swamp Angel does not Why don't you call the birds together to-night and challenge him to sing against you at a concert and allow them to decide once for all which is the sweeter singer?"

"Suppose they decide he is."

"That will be no worse for us than it will for them if the majority decides on you. Solomon Owl has the reputation of being the wisest bird, Jim Crow the smartest, and Quaker Dove the most tender and truthful. Go ask

120

them to come listen this evening, then arrange with Hermit to sing all your notes, one strain at a time, against each other and accept their decision as final   That will be perfectly fair to each of you, and I know who will win "

So Wood Robin arranged for the rival concert, and that evening when the latest rays of the sun fell in long, red banners of light across the water while all the woods were quiet, he hopped from branch to branch of the elm tree peering across the bay and listened intently.   At last he fluffed his feathers, lifted his beak, swelled his throat and softly. oh, so softly sent this challenge over the water: "Uoh?   Uoh?"

Among the ferns across the purple water a soft wind carried the answer. indescribably sweet and faint. "O fear all!"   Then stronger and clearer· "O fear all!" Then clear, high, cool and passionless from the button-bush that was his home rang the notes "O fear all!"

Wood Robin's challenge was answered.   He lifted his shoulders, his wing butts pressed his sides, his throat swelled fuller.

"Ā-ē-ō-l-ĭ!"   Lovingly rounding, fulling, accenting each vibrant note he spelled it out with utmost care.

Immediately the Hermit raised to his pitch, and through the damp green silence of the wood, evenly, clearly, with molten sweetness, poured the answer "Oh, u-ō-lēē!   Oh, u-o-lee!"

"Nōh, no!"   flung back Wood Robin's silver-bell-toned voice.

MORNING FACE

"Oh, klĕr-ah-wàh! Klĕr-ah-wah!" rolled the serene, piercing sweetness of the Hermit.

Wood Robin's knees stiffened. His beak parted farther. He bent far toward his rival, and sweeter than the finest golden-toned flute struck his notes: "Ā-ē-ō-lēē, lēē, lēē! Ā-ē-ō-lēē, lēē, lēē!"

Then with a tense shiver he listened

High, pure and clear, across the little bay swept the Hermit's melody. "O klĕr-ah! O klĕr-ah!"

Wood Robin stretched to his utmost height, filled his lungs and swelled his breast, pointed his beak Heavenward and in mellow cadence, rising higher and higher to piercing, painful sweetness, and then tenderly caressing each tone in the golden throat, he sank to a whisper and silence "Uŏli? Uŏli? Ā c-ō-le! Nŭll, nŏl! Ā-e-ō-lēē! lēē! lēē!"

The Hermit gripped the twig he stood on, tucked his tail, lifted his beak, and in calm, even tones of pure serene sweetness, with delicate prelude, shaking trills and throbbing melody, poured his full strain in answer, "Oh fear all! Fear all! Oh ū-ō-lēē! Oh ū-ō-lēē! O klĕr-ah-wäh! O klĕr-ah-wäh! O klĕr-ah! Klĕr-ah!"

Wood Robin closed his beak and hopping to a lower branch went before the judges for the decision A little later he returned to Bell who anxiously awaited the answer.

"Have they agreed?" she chirped.

"They have all agreed," answered Wood Robin slowly.

"The future of the Wood Robin family."

"They are unanimous?"

"Yes."

"And it is——"

"They have decided that I can beat him on colour and richness of tone, but that he has a serene purity that I cannot surpass "

"Lee, Lee!" cried Bell   "I think that is lovely   Now neither of you can boast over the other   That means that some will like one of your songs better while some will care most for the other "

"That is what it means," replied Wood Robin.

BABY FLICKERS

"THEY are climbing up the old dead tree,
Every minute going quicker,
I don't want them to get away,
But Gene says: 'Let them flicker!'"

125

" Gene, take me up and sing about 'Nestin'.' "

NESTIN'

"Oh MARY, me darlin', 'tis a bright April morn,
  Oh Mary, accushla, I'm so glad ye were born!"
"Oh Robin, me laddie, fair is the day,
  Oh Robin, ye blarney, I like what ye say!"

CHORUS DUET

"Heigh-lo, heigh-oh, Spring ever is fine,
  Heigh-ho, heigh-lo, young blood flows like wine.
  There's always a bird and a tree that's too high,
  While Robin and Mary are just you and I."

THRUSH CHORUS

"Aeole, hiole, hilo, hilee,
  Holy-a-olee, hi-oh-a-li-lee,
  Oh-lee, heigh-oh-lee, a-o-lee, li, lee,
  Holy, a-oh-lee, li-oh-li-lee-lee!"

127

MORNING FACE

"Come where the bell bird and the wild dove
  Are straining their throats with telling their love!"
"Sure, swate is the song-bird, fine is the flower,
  I'll go with ye laddie, for one little hour."

CHORUS

"Now Mary, accushla, watch each budding tree,
  And tell me, you darlin', what 'tis that you see!"
"In every tree, building 'round her own breast,
  Oh Robin, me laddie, a bird weaves her nest!"

CHORUS

"Oh Mary, me darlin', in the wood love is free,
  Oh come now, me sweetheart, be nestin' for me'"
'How can I, ye rascal, when trees are so high,
  How can I be buildin' up twixt earth and sky?"

CHORUS

"Oh Mary, me darlin', me soul sings with glee,
  Oh Mary, me darlin', I'll cut down the tree!"
"With joy like the birds, and with song like them too,
  Then Robin, me laddie, I'll be nestin' for you!"

CHORUS

THE COUNTRY LIFE PRESS
GARDEN CITY, N. Y.